STUDIES IN SEMIOTICS

edited by Thomas A. Sebeok
 Research Center for Language and Semiotic Studies
 Indiana University

Volume 17

ANNEMARIE LANGE-SEIDL

APPROACHES TO THEORIES FOR NONVERBAL SIGNS

LISSE
THE PETER DE RIDDER PRESS
1977

001.56
L26a

© Copyright 1977   Annemarie Lange-Seidl

No part of this book may be translated or reproduced in any form, by print, photoprint, microfilm, or any other means, without written permission from the author.

ISBN 90 316 0145 4

Photoset in Malta by Interprint (Malta) Ltd.
Printed in Holland by Intercontinental Graphics Dordrecht

Preface

I wish to thank the editor of the German original, Professor Dr. Brigitte Schlieben-Lange, for agreeing to produce the English version,
 the publishers Hoffmann und Campe Verlag Hamburg for granting the licence to do so,
 and Dr. Donald Gutch (Universität Regensburg) for offering suggestions which have helped to make the text sound more English.

Table of Contents

Preface 5

Introduction 9

1. The Attitude of Linguists 11

2. Sign Theories Independent of Language: Semiotics — Semiology 13

3. Linguistics as a Pilot Science (*patron général*) of Semiology . . 15
   3.1 Minimal Units 15
   3.2 Dichotomies, Trichotomies, the Code Concept, and Planes of Articulation 19
   3.3 Generative Aspects 21
   3.4 Sociolinguistics 22
   3.5 Psycholinguistics 22
   3.6 Pragmatics 24
   3.7 Objections to Linguistic Methods 24

4. Interdisciplinary Connexions 27
   4.1 Medicine and Biology 27
   4.2 Psychology 28
   4.3 Philosophy 29
       4.3.1 Epistemology and Logic 30
       4.3.2 Phenomenology and Symbolism 31
       4.3.3 Aesthetics and Functionalism 33
   4.4 Sociology 34

5. Basic Considerations 35
   5.1 Meaning and Sign 35
   5.2 Symptomatology – Sign Science 36
   5.3 Notation, Conservation, and the Media. 38
   5.4 Systems, Norms, and Principles 39
   5.5 Sign Competence 41
   5.6 Theoretization 42

Notes 43

References 49

Index of Names 57

Introduction

1. General sign science at the moment is doubtful about the "imperialism of language" (Jakobson 1974) among sign systems, in view of the profuseness of nonverbal signs in mathematics as well as in arts.
2. Linguistic methods and theories are nowadays often used for nonverbal sign systems as well. How far this is admissible must be investigated.
3. From theories for nonverbal signs and from general deliberation about what a sign is, new ideas for language theories may be gained.[1]

At the moment, the following starting points for theories of nonverbal signs can be stated:

1. By most linguists, nonverbal signs are either completely ignored or associated with language as the most important sign system. In recent studies oriented towards pragmatics, indications of a paralinguistic component of language are published.
2. Semiology as an independent sign science sees language as a special faculty of communication or of sign-giving (the two should not be identified, but can have areas in common); for the semiologist, linguistics is part of a comprehensive sign science, the part in which methodology and theoretization have made by far the most progress.
3. Linguistics has been taken as the pilot science (Solomon Marcus), "le patron général" (Saussure) of every semiological investigation. The methods of structuralism are considered with reference to nonverbal signs in a consistent way by semiologists; but semiotists hesitate at recent developments in linguistics.

4. For theoretization, methods and theories from categories and trends from mathematics, biology, medicine, psychology, sociology, as well as from cultural sciences, which have to consider nonverbal signs, are employed.

5. Starting from new basic reflections about meaning and sign, notation, conservation, mediation of signs, their combination in sign systems and their possible functions, sign competence would have to be considered and linked to action theories.

1

The Attitude of Linguists

Most linguists obviously shrink from thinking about nonverbal signs: Are there not problems enough with human language; have we not spent sixty years since Saussure classifying these problems, keeping heuristic principles apart from pragmatic claims, confronting socio- and psycholinguistic starts with methods from natural sciences? The theoretical discussion on the borders of logic and communication sciences is still ahead of us. The interdisciplinary interlacings which result in connection with the investigation of nonverbal signs are unlimited. Linguists fear a dilution of the clear demarcations they have just gained.[2]

On the one hand nonverbal signs have a tendency to move away from natural language into the range of formulae and symbols as a result of complicated human thinking processes, but they move as well toward technical experiments in communication sciences, across the borders of human communication into the much discussed area of animal signals and capacity for communication.[3] Here, the European linguist objects that animal signs are not arbitrary and therefore cannot be measured by language categories.[4] American semiotics, having grown up side by side with behaviorism and partly merging with it, take an attitude based less on philosophical considerations. For our purposes animal communication is not relevant, for we are dealing with human nonverbal systems, not with understanding between man and animal, or among animals.

The scruples against such an extension of the language problem into the domain of artificial constructs on the one hand, and into the field of nonhuman communication on the other, result in a conscious trend toward non-positivistic philosophy among linguists, and together with this a reflection on what is typical of man: man's capacity for reflection; the lie as a result of the conscious handling of language signs and the programming of human speech[5]; man's capacity to bring forth past and future references in his language, and to speak about his language.

Nearly all linguists agree that the concept 'language' must be kept in reserve for human verbal language and must not be used for nonverbal systems.[6]

"Sensoric communication modalities"[7] are graded as a matter of subordinate importance, as they are said not to constitute constant systems. They are conceded to individuals[8] or types as "indexical characteristics" and are considered as reactions to speech and writing.[9]

'Prosody and the paralinguistic component': Vigor of voice, timbre, stress, pauses and speech velocity, facial expression, the gestures and physical bearing which accompany speech are evaluated either as the "prosodic component of a language system"[10] or as signs accompanying speech, which can, but need not, be isolated, and are comprehended by the name 'paralinguistic component'.[11] Though rated rather high by Birdwhistell (1961) with 65–70% of the social significance of a discourse or interaction, they are only gradually being noticed at all as a component of speech by recent linguistic papers oriented towards pragmatics. We must ask ourselves whether the commentaries of colloquial speech do not manifest themselves paralinguistically by nature, whether a transfer to verbal discourse, to utterances in metalanguage, is really to be evaluated as an elucidation (cf. Lange-Seidl 1976b).

2

Sign Theories Independent of Language: Semiotics — Semiology

Elisabeth Walther (1974) published a "Survey of the History of Semiotics from Plato up to the Present" (pp. 9–43). Therefore we can confine ourselves to a few notes, which we shall refer to further on. We wish to call attention to Alain Rey (1973) and Achim Eschbach's bibliographies as well. The non-linguistic sign theories are usually traced back to John Locke's *Essay Concerning Humane Understanding* (1690/1960, Book III). He proposed the name 'semiotic' for a science of signs and notations. Since Elisabeth Walther edited an excerpt from Bolzano's *Wissenschaftslehre* (1837/1971), the latter's sign concept has again been noticed in Germany. Bolzano demanded simple signs like those of mathematics for all domains in order to provide quick surveys or to avoid language redundancy. These signs should be easy to represent, free from secondary notions and clearly distinguishable. "If it is a fault to use now this, now that sign for one concept" – we should rather say: for the same proceedings or states of affairs – "it would be a more serious fault to have fewer signs than concepts" (Bolzano 1971, p. 46). Bolzano strictly rejected a purely metaphorical use of signs. What Walther took for 'pragmatics' with Bolzano, we prefer to take as the basic heuristic element of sign, as Bolzano himself did. Bolzano distinguished natural, fortuitous, and arbitrary signs as basic elements of logic, language, and heuristics, as things that refer to something else, in order to renew the latter in a thinking being. For Bolzano, the objective idea was the meaning of sign.

For Ferdinand de Saussure, language was only a special system within a universal science of signs, which he was the first to call 'semiology' in

November 1894. For him linguistics was only part of that science; and in his opinion, the laws that semiology would discover would be applicable to linguistics as well.[12] It is to be regretted that Saussure's initiative towards a general semiology has not produced semiological schools and tendencies for sixty years in the way that his suggestions for the synchronic consideration of speech and language have since been a stimulus for linguists.

In 1897, Charles Sanders Peirce used 'semiotic' in the sense of John Locke.[13] He distinguished icons, indices, and symbols, and thus was the first to try to define not only the characteristic features of signs, but sign itself as a special categorial entity in relation to, and in opposition to, some other entity (cf. Walther 1974, p. 44). Peirce finally reduced his original 59049 types of signs to 66 types, which, in Germany, Max Bense adopted and amplified as a "basic theory" for a general sign science.[14] One could adopt Elisabeth Walther's view putting Peirce's concept of meaning near what Bolzano had called the language interpretation ("sprachliche Auslegung"), that is a proposition which says something about the meaning of certain signs (cf. Walther 1971, p. 12).

In his glossary to "Signs, Language and Behavior", where Morris (1946) first claimed a "comprehensive doctrine of signs", he distinguished 'semiosis', as the process by which something becomes a sign for an organism, from 'semiotic'. The linguist is confused by Morris' classification of semiotic (1938) in the following way: 'syntactic' for the relations between sign and sign, 'semantic' for relations between sign and thing, 'pragmatic' as the reference of signs to "elicited behavior".[15] In his definition, 'pure semiotic' aims at a language in which one can speak about signs; 'descriptive semiotic', however, studies real signs; 'applied semiotic' uses this knowledge for certain different purposes. For Morris, pure semiotic, i.e. finding a terminology, and maybe a theory connected with it, stands temporally before sign description. According to Morris (1964, p. 1) "semiotic has for its goal a general theory of signs in all their forms and manifestations, whether in animals or men, whether normal or pathological, whether linguistic or nonlinguistic, whether personal or social. Semiotic is thus an interdisciplinary enterprise."[16]

3

Linguistics as the Pilot Science (*patron général*) of Semiology

Saussure conceded to linguistics that it could become the *patron général* of semiology, though language was only a special system in a general sign science.[17] Luis Prieto (1966a) kept up the range of Saussure's concept of semiology and suggested transferring linguistic theories to nonverbal signs and paving the way for an elucidation with their help. He himself tried out Saussure's classifications for nonverbal systems. In *Messages et signaux* (1966b) he systematically studied the significant and significate, seme and code of nonverbal signs in their logical correlations and mechanisms of function and economy.

Hjelmslev's concept of semiology as the teaching of meaning refers to the content-plane of language, not to nonverbal signs as one might conclude from the English version.[18]

In the following paragraphs I shall try to show where the procedures of linguistics have been transferred to semiology and examined as to their usefulness. Conversely, with reference to each single procedure we shall consider what nonverbal signs could offer to linguistics.

3.1 MINIMAL UNITS

According to Saussure (1916/1962, p. 157), one of the basic rules for structural linguistics was to isolate a concept from the system it is part of ("isoler un terme du système dont il fait partie"). The isolation of minimal units in a system of double articulation has also been taken over as a first step by semiology.

Stokoe (1960) used 'chereme' as an equivalent for phoneme in the gesture system of American deaf-mutes, 'allocher' as an equivalent for allophone, 'sign' as an equivalent for word, and 'gesture' for an unanalysed unit of communication (cf. Stokoe 1972, p. 20).

For paralinguistics, the smallest units for the distinction of meaning are: measurable voice intensity, measurable pauses, measurable gestures. Birdwhistell (1952, 1961) emphasized that, in such studies, biological aspects of behavior had to be strictly separated from the communication requirements of a certain society (1961, p. 93). He believed that only 30–35% of the social importance of a conversation or interaction was conveyed verbally.

In paralinguistics, biological data must be strictly distinguished from intentionality affected by situation. Only after eliminating organic failure may we consider that, in a small room, a loud voice has a meaning; in a large room, however, it is simply a condition for being understood. The reverse holds for a low voice. It is much more difficult to measure and isolate voice timbre than voice intensity. Nevertheless, we must try to get hold of it in its social and communicative significance.

Pauses are measurable, but it is difficult to separate pauses affected by biological conditions and speech competence from those whose effect has been considered in advance (cf. Goldman-Eisler 1968).

Kinetics has motion as its principle (Popper 1967, p. XV). It provides the methods for the description of all body motion, as well as for all artistic motion.

Birdwhistell (1952) formed the expression 'kineme' for the smallest motion distinguishing meaning and in 1970, as a result of his investigations, set up 32 kinemes in the area of face and head (p. 99). In his opinion, these kinemes may be combined to formal 'kinemorphs', from which kinemorphic classes may be analysed "which behave like morphemes" (p. 101). Birdwhistell does not, however, believe that gestures can be isolated from forms of behavior, the functions of which they determine in a process of interaction (p. 80).

How far we may consider elements and directions of motion as distinctive for meaning, and their relations as carriers of meaning, i.e. how far we can take into consideration double articulation in the sense of Martinet, has not yet been sufficiently investigated. If we could really isolate them as far as we think we are able to isolate language elements from social and personal relationship, we could call the science of kinemes and kinemorphs 'kinemics'[19] and thus set it apart from 'kinetics', which has always been oriented psychologically, as well as from Birdwhistell's 'kinetics', which is related to biology and physiology. The modern tendency in visual art to make use of motion signs would then have a better semiological foundation.

'Proxemics' tries to apply linguistic methods to space relations. Edward T. Hall, who first used the name 'proxemics', has since had great difficulties in classifying 'proxes', 'alloproxes', and actually distinctive 'proxemes' as minimal units in a synchronic comparison of different cultures (Hall 1963, p. 1022). Hall himself admitted that his investigations have more the character of 'proxetics' than 'proxemics' (p. 1021). His opinion was that 'proxemics' completely corresponds to language, but is less specialized (p. 1019). We must ask ourselves whether, according to Hall, 'proxemics' is space behavior or the science of space behavior. Knowledge of the relations of language to other cultural systems is fluid for Hall: while language is taken too much as an instrument for communication, proxemics is reduced to transaction between groups and their surroundings: "That makes it difficult to relate proxemics at all significant levels to current linguistic models" (p. 1021).

If, with great reservation, we transfer the principle of double articulation to proxemics, we could consider measurable distance and measurable expansion as distinguishing meaning; reduction of distance by motion, reduction of expansion by motion, increase of distance by motion, increase of expansion by motion as bearing meaning. Hall had no suggestions for clear distinctions between his proxemes.

Semiology will have to begin with narrowly confined single cultures like the comparison of Neapolitan gestures with West Indian ones by Wilhelm Wundt (1921, 1973) or the comparison of gestures in the Jewish Ghetto and in the Sicilian immigrant quarter in New York by David Efron (1941/1971). But we will not be able to deal with such vast areas as the USA and the Arab world or the Far East, as Hall tried to in his proxemic research.

The Conference on Architectural Psychology in Dalandhui 1969 discussed the concept 'environics'. The claims laid down by them correspond to Hall's definition of proxemics (1963, p. 1003): "Proxemics, the study of how man unconsciously structures microspace — the distance between men in the conduct of daily transactions, the organization of space in his houses and buildings, and ultimately the layout of his towns." But the architects want to replace the expression 'unconsciously' by a conscious consideration of space demands by man for his functions of living, working, display; they require single houses and groups of buildings, planned according to these claims, especially in future city-planning. So, where space units are in question, American semiotics has already taken on international and interdisciplinary importance, though the investigations of the biological and material prior conditions of nonverbal behavior, as compared with language, only allow an association with phonetics, but not with structural linguistics or with the semiology claimed by Saussure.

If we use 'kinetics' for biologically involved movements of the human body, and 'kinesics' for fundamental investigations of the principle of motion, 'kinemics', however, for systems of movements the meaning of which is clear to all men or only to single groups or cultures; if 'proxemics' examines when and how spatial proximity or spatial distance have a meaning for single persons, for groups, or for cultures, or may be used consciously by them; then we will be obliged to take the name 'proxetics' for much that has gone under the name 'proxemics' in recent years. According to this procedure, we could, and would have to, distinguish more exactly between the scientific prior conditions for signs, which semiotics deals with, and the social and action-theoretic problems of sign, in the sense of semiology.

For music, Pierre Schaeffer (1966) tried an application of linguistic methods which is not convincing. For Schaeffer, music and language both consist of sound and both develop in time (p. 284). Therefore they may be measured by the same categories. Schaeffer did not contribute to a sign theory specific to music.

For photography, Lindekens (1971) distinguished *l'objet iconisé* as a distinctive minimal unit from the *objet verbalisable* as unit of identification. He distinguished the scrutinizer of a photograph, who comprehends the sense, from the reader, who comprehends the meaning (p. 97).

As theoreticians of film, Sol Worth and Christian Metz should be quoted here, because they try to apply linguistic principles and aim to find minimal units.

For film semiotics, Sol Worth (1969) provided a number of minimal units, but not in the sense of double articulation. A 'videme' is a shot which corresponds to the image event, a 'cademe' a shot which corresponds to the will of the cameraman, including the limits imposed by technics. An 'edeme' is a shot actually used for presentation (p. 300). We must bear in mind that these units are in reality abbreviations for technical procedures, not minimal units isolated theoretically in the sense of structuralism.

Christian Metz (1971) is the most thoroughgoing of film theoreticians to examine the elements of linguistic structuralism concerning their possible application to the theoretization of what is typical in film. The avantgardists of film have been in touch with each other from the beginning, and by applying the most recent scientific knowledge, have tried to employ optical media consciously, being thoughtful of leaving the spectator in the dark about the origin of the effect of the film. Metz rejected the search for minimal film units by Sol Worth, Pier Paolo Pasolini, and Gianfranco Bettetini, because they could only be relevant for a certain film code, but never for film as a whole. Metz believes neither in the existence of a cinematographic sign, nor in minimal relevant film units. He takes distinctive features smaller than every given sign for the typical possibilities of film.

3.2 DICHOTOMIES, TRICHOTOMIES, THE CODE CONCEPT AND PLANES OF ARTICULATION

Semioticians pay less attention to sign-giving as the equivalent for speech (*parole*) than to the description of systems. Linguists energetically oppose the use of the notion 'language' (*langue*) for systems which do not correspond to double articulation (Martinet) and for systems of expression or communication which are not accomplished in a linear and verbal way. To approach the faculty of sign-giving, semiotists frequently return to Saussure's concept of *langage*, i.e. the faculty of speech, which was kept in the background during the domination of structuralism and has only been brought into play again by psycholinguists. Thus Metz (1971) restricted the use of *langue* to verbal language, as far as it is used in sound-film, and took *langage*, i.e., the faculty of speech, for the film itself.

The dichotomy paradigmatic/syntagmatic has hardly ever been used for nonverbal signs. For film, it was rejected by Metz.

According to Metz (1973, p. 175), film sequences, which could be considered syntagmata (Sol Worth compared them with morphemes), do not reach the spectator's perception, as one sequence is followed by the next one, and each of them has both a different content-substance and a different type of construction.

Semiologists disagree regarding the use of code concepts from communication theory or linguistics[20]. For Metz, 'code' in the sense of communication theory meant a tool in the form of a system which could be re-used ad infinitum and which stood for the intrinsic instrumentality of art. He completely rejected linearity and double articulation for film. Nevertheless, this double articulation plane according to the linguistic model has been striven for by others in the nonverbal domain.

For film, Sol Worth assumed a triple structure of parameters: content aspects like picture, motion, time, space, order; technical aspects like cut, fade-over, fading; and sensoric aspects like the film sequence. These parameters might be regarded as a structuralistic starting-point for film theory. Several times Sol Worth stressed his reference to linguistics, made use of the notion 'language' for the nonverbal elements of film, and asked if a 'universal language of film', which would depend on the general faculty of man to perceive and code iconic pictures, could be taken for granted.

It is Umberto Eco's opinion, too, that in contrast to the double articulation of language a triple cinematographic articulation should be assumed. He includes chronological order and the total motion inside the picture as the third articulation plane of film. This could be maintained for verbal speech as well, if paralinguistic motion elements in certain spatial communication situations were included.

Contrary to Sol Worth's triple articulation plane for the sequence and Eco's inclusion of the time dimension, Wunderlich (1971, p. 159) believed he could reduce film kinetically and proxemically to a double system of presentation. He distinguished the kinetic presentation, as a spatial change independent of external conditions, from the dynamic presentation, which is defined by causes and intentions of motion. What Wunderlich called 'dynamics' could be called 'kinemics' in the case of single movements and 'dynamics' in the case of sequences and complexes belonging to the character of a person or situation. But the kinemic presentation, which makes motion signs conscious, could be inserted too between kinetics and dynamics. For Wunderlich (1971), 'syntax' meant the total composition structure of a film (p. 60); for the 'semantics' of a film he separated the plane of the cameraman's perceptions from the plane of the spectator's interpretation of the finished film (p. 160). It is not clear where the use of conscious cinematographic signs or elements is to be inserted. Wunderlich mentioned a 'metalanguage' of film (1971, p. 161), and, as an example, quoted the concept 'induced motion': static picture elements can receive sign status by the camera motion or disappear from sign status to insignificance without moving themselves.

Metz advised a descriptive film semiology and warned against too normative a conception of semiology. He saw the single film as a *totalité singulière*, as a hermeneutic unit, which, like a text, gains its final meaning by the perception of each individual recipient.

Spatial-temporal production events and psychological laws for production do not play too important a role in a purely structural film theory, on which linguistics has had great influence. Though many film theoreticians tested structuralistic methods with open minds, sign theory for film should rather be associated with perception aesthetics than with linguistic structuralism, for film production is a complicated system of intentionality on the part of the script writer, the producer, the director, the assistants, the actors and the cameraman, and of interpretation by the stage team and the cutter, which may lead to technical interventions. For perception, the interpretation by the individual spectator plays as decisive a role as does the interpretation by the mass of spectators who happen to be present.

3.3 GENERATIVE ASPECTS

Too little attention has been paid to the 'performance' of nonverbal signs. We may ask ourselves by what right elocution training groups with the help of video-recorders decide which face motion or gesture was right or wrong in which situation, i.e. how far the speaker's competence in nonverbal signs goes, as long as there are no norms for nonverbal signs. If, following Chomsky's example, we leave situation out of the question, the application of 'competence' to nonverbal signs becomes still more absurd.

For education at conservatories and academies of art, the use of models always went without saying. It was, however, associated with practical training, not with theoretical education. May we assume real sign competence only in art? Or, conversely: is the complete control of a communication event already art? Or artificial? As long as we believe in the unconscious use of nonverbal communication elements and not in intention concerning semiosis, we cannot use the notion 'competence'. Only after having once more considered the essential features of a sign, only after a theoretical reorientation will the notion 'sign competence' be used with justice. The prior condition for a system that is formalizable and formalized is that the notation and conservation of signs are normalized and standardized (cf. p. 38 and 39f).

Susan H. Houston (1972) claimed for generative grammar that it should have a semantic or message component and moreover a pragmatic or medium component (p. 227)[21]; she included extralinguistic phenomena, especially paralinguistic features like velocity of speech, length of utterances, phenomena of retardation, voice quality, and rhythm. In her opinion, these elements of the component would have to be 'acceptable' and 'formalizable'. It is not clear enough what Houston meant by the notion 'medium'. Does the acceptability refer not to the component itself, but to the elements? Are these made conscious? Then we no longer have an unconscious component by which the hearer can conclude as to the speaker's seriousness, state of health, and humor from gestures and voice timbre, which would not have been revealed in consciously motivated and directed speech (p. 228). Here there is a contradiction, in my opinion: a formalizable system will always be at the same time a conscious one, the elements of which may be inserted as arbitrary signs.

3.4 SOCIOLINGUISTICS

Up to now, sociolinguistics has not been taken into consideration as a starting-point for nonverbal sign theories. A sociosemiology will have to consider, if, like sociolinguistics, it is to depict diatopic, diastratic, and diaphasic differences (Flydal, Coseriu, Schlieben-Lange[22]), what persons and groups in what roles and situations require and use more nonverbal signs than verbal ones. The preference for signs of different kinds will have to be studied, as well as the priorities of nonverbal and verbal signs. Extralinguistic phenomena may be restricted to the idiolect; then they are to be evaluated as symptoms, not as conscious signs for other persons; but they may also be peculiarities of a certain 'dialect', of a language group, of one or several cultures.

Houston (1972) is right to stress that the hitherto prevailing neglect of extralinguistic components in cultures may, by a lack of appreciation, cause serious misunderstandings in a total communication situation, often with grave international consequences (p. 228).

3.5 PSYCHOLINGUISTICS

Let us condense psycholinguistics and take the following areas as a basis:
 1. events of coding and decoding;
 2. reception and perception of speech utterances;
 3. production of speech and language;
 4. acquisition and loss of speech and language;
 5. comparisons within one language system and among several systems on a psychological basis;

6. efficiency and effect of speech or of a language system (cf. Lange-Seidl 1972/1973).

We will then arrive at the following results and suggestions for nonverbal sign theories:

1. The multiplicity of signs (acoustic, optical, proxemic, kinemic, olfactory, motoric signs) has up to now complicated the clear isolation and comprehension of codes, and of events of encoding and decoding.
2. For a long time psychology has dealt with sensoric perception problems.[23] The transition from reception to perception and, *vice versa*, from perception to conception has been difficult to grasp in all sensoric domains.[24]

   While Schaeffer (1966) suggested the four levels *écouter, ouïr, entendre, comprendre* for the musical perception process, Lindekens (1971) made the distinction of the four grades *regarder, voir, apercevoir, comprendre* for the optical perception process. We must ask ourselves if this perception process in four grades holds for hearing and reading too, if, depending on the use of a primary or a secondary medium, language must be taken as an acoustic or optical sign process. The planes of perception have received much less attention by linguistics than those of articulation have.
3. The multiplicity of nonverbal signs involves a multiplicity of production processes, which up to now have mainly been investigated in the artistic disciplines. No suggestions from psycholinguistics have been taken up.
4. German school curricula are not concerned with the acquisition of nonverbal signs. In the secondary schools, the acquisition of language systems prevails; in professional schools the acquisition of motor skills predominates.

   Aphasia research has long since taken into account the correlations between the loss of the faculty of speech (*langage*), the loss of language perception, and the loss of the faculty of producing nonverbal signs belonging to the communication process.[25] The aphasia investigations in hospitals and asylums need to be complemented by investigations into the healthy person's partial or complete loss of sign capacity under different physiological and psychological prior conditions; into his behavior under the influence of drugs, and also into the conditions under which a human being is inclined to an abnormally increased use of signs, to which his fellow-creatures' reaction is considerably more sensitive than to sign economy or sign restriction.

5. System comparisons have been made in kinemics and proxemics.
6. Without improved consciousness and knowledge, the efficiency of sign perception and semiosis is not to be judged. As regards sign effect, we stand at the crossroads of conscious, almost manipulative semiosis and unconscious sign reception, doggedly maintained. The question should be broached as to how far habituation overlaps with interpretation, and this question would have to be stressed consciously and theoretically for the effect of nonverbal signs. Till now such studies were to be found in the domain of aesthetics (cf. Umberto Eco: *Opera aperta* and *Struttura assente*). In a kind of sign rhetoric,[26] sign effects and their methods could be comprehended. This sign rhetoric would stretch from the domain of psychology into that of pragmatics. But we must ask ourselves if this knowledge will not be hermetically shielded from the public for ever, as too great a transparency could reduce the effect of signs instead of increasing it.

3.6 PRAGMATICS

Within linguistics pragmatics turns the sign concept into an action concept (cf. Schlieben-Lange 1975). Here sign science will have to find a position, for its interests are far less apt to be isolated from actions than language signs are. Sign scientists will have to explore where speech acts and the 'concept reference' (cf. Searle 1969) have their analogies in the nonverbal domain.[27] The differences between natural and institutional facts, which Searle investigated for speech acts, concern the nonverbal domain too. Searle's reproaches against the paralogisms of modern language philosophy would have to be considered for a theory of nonverbal signs as well. The studies attached to pragmatics might be rather productive for corresponding theories in the nonverbal domain; but there is the risk that sign science attached to action would irreversibly reduce its descriptive phase for the benefit of action theories and that, thereby, sign science would lose distinctness and precision.

3.7 OBJECTIONS TO LINGUISTIC METHODS

So far we have presented attempts and suggestions aimed at arranging a general sign science according to the model of linguistics which already exists. But one may also criticize such a proceeding.

Mounin (1970) considers it dangerous to use linguistic concepts and terms without caution, and to apply them for nonverbal sign systems beyond a first operational hypothesis. At a certain stage of theoretization, we must realize that painting does not function like language, which will lead us to the necessary independent research methods. Mounin believes that social psychology and sociology may give much more help for comparisons among the individual disciplines of semiology and for its theoretization than linguistics. He refuses to talk about 'Klee's vocabulary', 'Mondrian's grammar', and 'Kandinsky's syntax' (cf. p. 225). He warns against equating 'non-linguistic' with 'ideographic' (p. 20). Elisabeth Walther (1974) claims that all attempts at a transfer of linguistic methods to semiotic methods will fail (p. 142), as linguistics is not a general sign theory but itself requires a foundation in a general sign theory (cf. Lange-Seidl 1975b).

We must ask ourselves, too, if a sign theory determined by the model of linguistics could solve all the problems connected with signs, or could even begin to treat them. Therefore the interdisciplinary connexions of general sign science must now be examined.

4

Interdisciplinary Connexions

Let us now consider in which disciplines sign-scientific questions are treated or should be treated and whether the results could be used as impulses for a general sign theory.

4.1 MEDICINE AND BIOLOGY

In German encyclopaedias, you may find *Semiotik*, in Romance countries *sémiologie* or *semiologia* as the term for a branch of medicine which, in English, has the more appropriate name *symptomatology*.[29] In medicine, we know of symptoms whose signal functions, released by steering processes in the brain, are examined by biology, e.g., swellings of tonsils and glands, coughing. The opinions on therapies diverge: (1) removal of the organ which bears the symptoms; (2) stabilisation of the circulation, improvement of the environmental conditions which caused the symptoms.

Beyond this, medicine knows conscious signs which are employed to correct physiological deficiency symptoms. For the blind, Braille developed a system of touch signs, which allows the blind to read texts and record messages themselves. While the Braille system has been institutionalized internationally, the gesture systems for deaf-mutes show cultural and national differences.[30]

The semiotician need not once more examine and describe the muscle areas which execute certain body movements. Physiology has provided such descriptions for centuries.[31] The task of sign science is rather to investigate the importance and the use of such movements.

In connection with proxemics, Hall examined the heat economy of the human body.[32] In fact, we have no means of controlling the heat of our body consciously and thereby using the radiations of heat as a sign. But it is possible to perceive and realize the responses to these symptoms. It is with much more consciousness that persons have tried to control the scent of the personal environment. Unconscious body odor is evaluated as a symptom by medicine; conscious body scent is fostered as a sign by the perfume industry. The North American reservedness concerning scent is culturally remarkable: every natural scent which could be symptomatic has to be suppressed rigorously by artificial means.[33]

Psychiatry has placed a lot of test results at the semiotician's disposal. We will have to select those of them which refer to an excess or to the loss of nonverbal sign use. We shall have to direct our attention to the intended and unintended movements of the sick body and the sick mind as well, but we must not forget that shock, stress, fatigue also have effects on sign perception and production. We tend to be more ready to conclude nervous defects from an excess of signs and from too hectic a semiosis than from too few signs. But the same holds for the verbal domain: the taciturn does not seem so defective to us as the too loquacious person, the chatterbox. For the psychiatrist, however, self-indulgence in semiosis, both verbally and nonverbally, constitutes a remedy for the restoration of psychological balance.[35]

4.2 PSYCHOLOGY

The consideration of equilibrium leads us into the very centre of psychology, to which Saussure wanted to attach a general sign science. According to Saussure,[36] the psychologist should have theoretical priority. The notion of 'balance' was one of the ideas of *Gestalttheorie*[37] which could still offer suggestions for a sign theory, especially for the perception process.[38]

'Gestalt' is seen as a totality standing out against a background, more or less closed and structured in itself, and transposable. A general sign science would have to oppose the Gestalt theoreticians' opinion that countless shapes cannot be reduced to elements according to the principles of structuralism. Research in 'apparent movements' could be fertile for kinemics. It will not be possible to reduce meaningful facial motion to a classification of moving and moved muscular areas; we must rather take up the impulses of Bühler's expression theory (*Ausdruckstheorie*, 1933).

The sensoric isolation of signs is difficult at a time in which the interaction of sense impressions and sense expressions is no longer evaluated as a symptom of mental derangement, but considered as an obvious device of style and consciously used by literature and advertising. The separation of space and time perception can no longer be strictly maintained now that the notion 'space-time' is used in physics (Einstein, Jacoby).

Psychology will have to help us to distinguish releasing signs from provoking ones, consoling signs from encouraging ones (cf. note 27). How do people become indifferent to signs because of their being used too often? The close connection of American semiotics with behaviorism can help us here; behaviorism may be instructive for the constitution, use and rejection of signs, but may not be so decisive that intentionality, meaning, and finality, which constitute the essence of the sign, should be neglected as is the case with many American studies.

By means of psychology and perception aesthetics we will have to distinguish natural sense impressions from culturally habitualized ones, as Hall did for the visual faculty in its consequences for space consciousness.[39]

It is open to question whether we may suppose a universal 'category of body language' as "a reflexion (of) constitutional factors ..., which is the same for all somatically normal individuals" (Diebold 1968, p. 537), whether universals of nonverbal communicative behavior are always "naïve and under less conscious control" (Diebold 1968, p. 544), i.e., universally innate, or whether signs are arbitrary in individual cultures.

4.3 PHILOSOPHY

I will now try to summarize what developments in the field of philosophical categories have contributed and are able to contribute to the elucidation of problems in the domain of nonverbal signs. Only as long as a sign-philosophic and sign-theoretic synopsis does not exist will one dare to speak about the 'prelingual' character of nonverbal signs. Sign competence is worth a theoretization as much as communicative competence, which cannot remain a lingual one, if it is not to ignore reality by being limited to a 'homo loquens'.

If, with Habermas (1970/1973), we distinguish 'rational reconstruction', which according to him linguistics aims at, from a communicative speaker's self-reflection of fundamental experiences in hermeneutics (p. 270), we come to the conclusion that nonverbal symptoms can be unconscious prior conditions, nonverbal signs conscious ones, but also unconscious and conscious results of accomplished efforts.

4.3.1 Epistemology and Logic

In epistemology and logic we are able to discern two fundamental extreme points of view:

(1) nonverbal signs belong to prelingual operative intelligence, on which language is superimposed (Habermas 1970/1973, p. 274);

(2) nonverbal signs belong to a grade of reflection[40] which develops symbols beyond language.

(1) Impulses for this conception often start from psychology, but are also related to pragmatism. To lay bare the language-independent roots of operative thinking was especially Jean Piaget's interest.[41] To put them to the test, Furth endeavoured to follow thinking processes without language in deaf-mutes.[42] Nonverbal sign theories will not be able to avoid arguing Piaget's notion of representation, which is for him an individual person's ability to make events present for himself which are not present in his senses. Piaget connects this ability with the semiotic function of intelligence. For him, language and iconic symbols are products of this ability, but never necessary elements for operative cognition; that means that for Piaget cognition is never only a matter of representation.[43] For Furth, every symbol has an operative and a figurative aspect and serves for equilibration, which, with Bertalanffy, he comprehends as the fluent equilibrium of an open system.[44]

Between the extremes 1 and 2, there is the operative foundation of logic offered by Lorenzen.[45] As he wants to make use of language as a didactic aid for the introduction of elements of the predicative calculus, without this language being a systematic condition, so the mediating role of language for the introduction and explanation of nonverbal signs would have to be studied more exactly for theoretization.

(2) For the second extreme standpoint I wish to quote two epistemologists as examples: Georg Klaus and L. O. Resnikow.

For Klaus, signs were not conceivable empirically, but always classes of abstraction. He distinguished the studies of nonverbal signs which immediately lead to a certain behavior and only require sense-perception[46] from the efforts to find signs containing messages for other persons, or storing knowledge which requires conscious reflection. That is what Klaus called a sign scheme, a pattern for action according to which arbitrarily new sign specimens could be produced which immediately after their production might disappear, as is the case in speech (Klaus 1963, p. 58).

Kamlah, too, used the notion "scheme of action, which we call sign in our language use" (Kamlah/Lorenzen 1967, p. 58 and 99).

It will have to be considered whether Klaus' sign classes and the action schemes of his sign shapes are to be regarded as "signs in zero situation"[47] or sign principles rendering new sign production possible. This 'abstract position' will certainly have to be taken into consideration for a theoretization, but the examples chosen by Klaus and his classification of signs seem to be more of a heuristic method than a step toward theoretization for a general sign science.

Resnikow (1964/1968) aimed at a general classification of sign systems, which in the sense of information theory serve to formalize scientific cognition.

4.3.2 Phenomenology and Symbolism

R. L. Lanigan (1972) studied the relations between communication theory and phenomenalism. The sign concepts of Peirce (p. 52), Morris (p. 54), Ogden and Richards (p. 58) are elucidated with Merleau-Ponty's categories and opposed to Jaspers' *chiffre* concept (p. 65) and Heidegger's sign concept (p. 71). According to Lanigan, "the sign is always a sign in use".

Husserl's opinion (*Logische Untersuchungen*, vol. 2) that paralinguistic elements should regulate the relations among words may be used for judging nonverbal signs.

The linking of psychological and philosophical disciplines to a symbolism like the one Susanne K. Langer developed in *Philosophy in a New Key* (1942) may be used as a starting-point for a theory of nonverbal signs. Langer started from Ritchie's opinion that thinking was a symbolic process in all its stages, and that the act of thinking essentially meant symbolizing. In her reflections, Langer included Cassirer,[50] Carnap, and Whitehead, and the literature on 'meaning' accessible at that time.[51] She thought man's world consisted much more of symbol and meaning than of sense-perceptions (1965, p. 35). For man is able to synthesize, retard, and modify his reactions by inserting symbols into the gaps and the confusion of experience, and by adding the experiences of other persons to his own with the help of verbal signs. Langer distinguished symptoms from symbols (1965, p. 39), which both had to be able to mediate meaning. The idea that the human brain continually translates experiences into symbols and thus carries out a constant 'process of ideation' as a 'principle of symbolizing' can be drawn on when considering whether thought processes without language are possible.

For Langer, symbolizing is preconceptual, but not irrational, and it is a starting-point for every kind of understanding in a specifically human sense. We probably will have to assume several stages in the process by which, in a dialectic change, ideation in Langer's sense and reflective conception follow each other. At every higher level, those degrees become more profound and abstract, until they are cultural symbols, as in the arts, or pure abstraction symbols, as in mathematics and logic.

Langer evaluated language as a natural result of only one kind of symbolic process, and believed in experience transformations in the human brain which manifest themselves in acts which are neither practical nor communicative, but can be as well effective as common.

Langer attacked the 'error' that every articulated symbolism is discursive (p. 94). We may retort that not all visual forms need be representative, as Langer thought and her present-day adherents tend to believe.

The distinction between temporal arts (literature, music) and spatial arts (painting, sculpture), which Lessing made in *Laokoon*, Chapter XV, in 1766, and which, stimulated by Langer's distinction between discursive and representative behavior, has recently reestablished itself, must not be stressed too much in the twentieth century, where for physics the indivisible space-time totality has been demonstrated (Einstein, Jacoby). A division into spatial signs and signs with linear and temporal character is helpful heuristically, but questionable theoretically.[52] For a rough distinction, the spatial problems of proxemics may be separated from the temporal problems of kinemics, but there is no punctual existence in space: he who moves in a time process moves in space, not in a vacuum. Especially for theater, music,[53] and film[54] it is foolish to draw a line, for they would then lose the space-time character which is a mark of the twentieth century.

4.3.3 Aesthetics and Functionalism

That philosophical aesthetic theories have to be considered in a general sign science goes without saying. But not every sign theory will have to be an aesthetic theory. In linguistics, aesthetic considerations nowhere occur; stylistics is rejected; nobody speaks of 'beautiful language'. For nonverbal signs, it will not be so easy to eliminate the aesthetic category, as in many cases the aesthetic factor decides the effect of the signs, even if it is in the sense of a 'negative dialectic'. The effect of the 'ugly' sign is very important for present art. The question of whether ugly gesture has a more repellent effect than ugly language needs to be studied. Ugly speech is not used as a negative factor as much as the ugly nonverbal sign.

Max Bense (1969) used the notion aesthetics in a different sense. His 'information aesthetics' is linked to technology and material; his numerical conception of aesthetics offers methods for computational techniques in graphic arts and architecture, in the sense of an abstract 'constation aesthetic', which relies chiefly on Birkhoff's aesthetic measure quotient $M_A = O/C$ (Bense 1969, p. 43). In the section on linguistics, we have referred to the double articulation of language and to its possible or not possible transferability to nonverbal signs; Bense, however, uses three-dimensionality, taken from Peirce: the triadic operation of signs (p. 10); the triadic function of signs (p. 11); the triadic operation of signs, which occurs as a linkage of single signs into sign chains (adjunction), as the iteration of the sign, as superisation of signs[55] into sign shapes and sign structures, and may be combined to form a triadic total scheme (p. 11).[56]

According to Bense, the conception of aesthetics developed by him has to be kept as an open system in research as well as in intention and in the domain of application. I am not sure whether this claim may be maintained independently of pressure groups, as their aim is not only the systematic description of the world, but the insight into the world's essential constructivity gained by this description, the systematic anticipation and programming of a future artistic reality (p. 71).

An analysis of the functions of nonverbal signs will have to be undertaken[57] and we will have to try to discover how far the function and the aesthetics of the sign reciprocate or are independent of each other.

Pierre Alexandre's opinion is that sign systems deprived of their practical function by a frequently occurring process tend to become art or play.[58] The editors of *rot*, a series of small books (ed. Elisabeth Walther,

Stuttgart), have investigated this transition from practical function to the aesthetic category. The uniform use of small letters in a German publication elucidates the disfunctionalization of capital letters and their refunctionalization as graphic ornaments with particular clarity.

Baudrillard (1972) followed the opposite method. In the Bauhaus he saw the start of a sign economy which liberated the sign from every religious, magic, symbolic, or traditional implication, and made it the object of a rational calculus of signification and thereby objectivized the total environment as an element of signification (p. 321).

4.4 SOCIOLOGY

For Saussure, the embedding in social relations was an obvious prior condition for semiology (Saussure 1916/1962, p. 3). It is astonishing that Mead, Goffman, and symbolic interactionalism have so far been too little noticed by semiotists.

For his proxemics, Hall[59] worked partially with sociological methods taken from statistics by neutralizing two factors in order to see how the third changed. He warned against not considering the social behavior of different cultures, which may manifest itself in nonverbal signs.[60]

5

Basic Considerations

We have endeavored to show approaches which are more or less usable, more or less developed and capable of development for the theoretization of nonverbal signs. We now wish to add some basic considerations.

5.1 MEANING AND SIGN

From the different conceptions of 'meaning', different standpoints for theories of nonverbal signs might result.

If meaning is content of possible interpretations, theories of nonverbal signs will have to be placed next to aesthetic and cultural theories; signs will have the function of presentation. If we understand meaning as intention, as meaningfully structured expectations (Habermas 1972, p. 119) which constitute themselves by reciprocal reflexivity, nonverbal signs would have to be assigned to action theories and would take on an appellative function. If meaning is conceived as the value which a certain thing has for one or several persons; if thereby it differs from being and is left to the freedom of interpretation and presentation; then the conscious sign used by the single person predominates, thus admitting temporal and personal grades of valuation. Here the sign is already an expression of such an assignment of meaning, which may be of an ethical or aesthetic nature, and has expressive function. Anthropology, phenomenology, and existentialism equate meaning and being; then signs are mediators of understanding, and can be a help for the interpretation of meaning.

If 'sign' is to be understood as only related to one object, only a small part of language can be considered a sign system. The expressive, representative and appellative functions (Bühler) need not be equated with the sign function. For sign comprehension, the following shift would be possible: if being and the contact of meaning are primary, signs — including verbal ones and thinking as the sum of several contents of meaning — are secondary. However, if signs are primary, then their mediation by speaking — that is, by moving the speech organs —, by drawing, and by body movements like gesture is secondary.

5.2 SYMPTOMATOLOGY – SIGN SCIENCE

We must strictly distinguish between unconscious symptoms and conscious signs.[61] The conscious signs must be distinguished according to the degree of appropriateness for functions, according to aesthetic and psychological criteria for arts and according to the degree of arbitrariness a nonverbal *signe arbitraire* may have. But we must keep in mind that the degree of consciousness may be different between partners: conscious sign-giving may meet conscious sign perception, conscious sign-giving may meet unconscious sign reception, unconscious symptom-giving may meet conscious sign perception. Robinson (1972, p. 114) assumed less arbitrariness with signs mediated organically and greater arbitrariness with signs artificially constructed.[62] You will be as aware of mime and gesture as you are aware of speech (he who has heard tape-recordings of it will be more aware of his own speech) or your own handwriting only if you practise professionally in front of a mirror, like a (film) actor or a mannequin. Most people lack the total feedback for their own movements.

Because we are familiar with the actor as a prototype of the ability to slip arbitrarily into roles which he not only fills up verbally but also semiotically in many ways, some semioticians consider the *signe arbitraire* available for lies (cf. Sampson 1972). He who learns to control his movements, he who employs proxemics consciously, can programme them like language, and with their help he is able to lie as he is by means of language. Bateson (1968) believed it was difficult for actors to be sincere and make a natural impression if they knew how to employ kinetic and paralinguistic factors with the degree of conscious control which many of us think we have over verbal language. The more actors endeavor to seem credible in their private lives, the more others mistrust them (p. 615).

In spite of possible consequences, we agree with Saussure's opinion, as regards semiology: "Les signes entièrement arbitraires réalisent mieux que les autres l'idéal du procédé sémiologique" (Saussure 1916/1962, p. 101). This is the point where we can no longer consider semiology a science of behavior, for teleological thought and action are difficult to explain in a behavioristic way. Intentionality raises sign science beyond semiotics.

Studies of the fundamental intention of nonverbal sign-giving will be important: is a verbal statement to be moderated or emphasized by it, or is it to be denied? Do we use the nonverbal sign in a speechless state, caused by desperation, pain, helplessness, or joy, because we succumb to a momentary aphasic disorder or because the nonverbal sign belongs to a deeper level of our consciousness? Or is the use of nonverbal factors then only a symptom, not a sign? Do we not intentionally try to fill the gap caused by the lack of a common verbal code by nonverbal signs? Are nonverbal signs to be warnings, orders, requests, or hints? Are these signs employed as supranational message codes, in technology, traffic, science, and the arts? We know of cultures where verbal and nonverbal signs may express opposite meanings at the same time (cf. Melbin 1974, p. 300).

Here we must stop for a moment: the official who, as a trustworthy representative of his nation, says "no" verbally and so *de jure*, makes himself understood by a wink, by shutting one eye, by touching money, by a manual gesture which may mean that a larger banknote tucked in the application form could change the whole matter. Which is more powerful here: the verbal statement or the nonverbal sign? Legally, the verbal statement is valid, as it can be written down and signed in a report. Deeper, however, is the effect of the gesture, which stands behind the verbal statement but is more transient. As all testimony and records must remain impossible, the official cannot remember having closed an eye or touched money. If eye-closing and money-touching are not plainly conventionalized in the culture in question, he may explain them by a draught, or a gnat, and the applicant has not the slightest evidence of having been invited to bribe. But the official or a colleague suddenly replacing him has evidence of the attempt at bribery.

Let me repeat: the question of the different levels of sign systems has not been broached at all; their capability of being recorded and their degrees of effectiveness must be studied.

5.3 NOTATION, CONSERVATION AND THE MEDIA

The prior condition for sign standardization and sign competence combined with it from the standpoint of legal recognition is the possibility of noting and conserving signs, and distinguishing them as to their form of mediation, before we offer them systematically in catalogues and encyclopedias. I want to stress that a general sign science certainly has to consider these aspects, but they are not yet to be valued as theories.

Attempts at notation and coding have been undertaken chiefly from the extremes. Stokoe and Furth (cf. n. 30) have recorded sign systems for deaf-mutes. Bouissac (1973) tried to approach consciously employed human motion where it appears in extreme concentration: in circus acrobatics, for which relatively isolated and observable sequences of movements have to be noted so as to be repeatable at any time (p. 12). Here and in the well-known notation systems for ballet we can discern different methods of conceiving sequences of body dynamics: (1) they are described in natural languages; (2) there are description proposals for direct sign notation; (3) these latter may use descriptions as a relay in the process of transfer. According to Bouissac, the intelligibility of these transcriptions depends on the practical and theoretical knowledge and the cultural category of the recipient.

It was a contradiction when Hall (1963) defined proxemics as the study of the unconscious structuring of human space, in order to serve the execution of everyday transactions, the spatial organization of buildings, working procedures, and city planning, but at the same time aimed at a system of notation (p. 1006) from which the Conference on Architectural Psychology has already drawn conclusions (cf. p. 17).

As a means of seeing man and things in different space and time perspectives and letting them speak and act non-verbally at the same time, film has had an opportunity of notation and conservation which must be evaluated more directly than the writing which records language. It is true that, especially for someone who is not busy in the process of its production, film is not to be surveyed as fast as the written text is. Film has the linear structure of language and music, but is closely bound up with space in a dynamic process, which at the same time fixes and conserves motion.[63]

Wunderlich (1971) proposed a distinction in the notation of nonverbal signs between the fixation of information content and their role in a sign system.

Sign theories should aim at an exact distinction between immediate media like speech, gesture, and mime; secondary media like writing, pictures, and signals; and tertiary media like Morse signals and electronic data systems.

5.4 SYSTEMS, NORMS, AND PRINCIPLES

There are already a considerable number of recorded and standardized nonverbal sign systems. Their intersubjective and interdisciplinary examinability is made more difficult by the variation in the prestige of nonverbal signs in various cultures: their use may provoke sanctions as well as their non-use. Single signs or complete systems may be attached to ideologies.[65] We can plainly distinguish cultures which restrict nonverbal signs from others which encourage them.

In industrial nations, nonverbal signs have considerably increased. It would be impossible, and a retrogression, to replace them by language, for this would impede international agreement. Every branch of technology has a complete ideographic system: architectural plans, circuit diagrams for telephone installation, assembly plans for radio and television sets, plans for motor vehicles and aeroplanes, construction plans for foreign licensees, assembly plans for furniture and prefabricated houses. As far as they are only object designations without symbolic use, we must associate them with an operative intelligence (cf. 30) which they apply to. But more complicated systems depend on so much efficiency in thought, verbal as well as nonverbal, in discourse and suggestion for improvement, comparisons with other systems, and the elimination of misleading signs, and on abstraction, that we must place them on a level of reflection which stands above a series of dialectic encounters between operative and verbal intelligence.

Mounin (1970) pointed out that we use much more personal information on watches, scales, instrument panels, slide rules, measuring vessels, tickets, tills, index-cards, statements of invoices and accounts, receipts, water, electricity and gas meters, and calculating machines every day, than we receive letters. He thought that for this reason we must develop a general semiology (p. 24). We could add that in most jobs we use numbers even more than we talk.[66]

The abundance of nonverbal sign systems which man is exposed to in the industrial age, which he has to work with every day, does not allow their evaluation as 'preverbal, plainly operative, prelinguistic', but demands an exact theoretical distinction between these systems according to the reflection levels underlying them and the degree of intelligence which was necessary to create them and which is necessary for their perception, as well as according to their degree of pragmatic content.

The relation between language and nonverbal sign systems needs to be discussed. How far does language play a decisive part in the conventionalization and the acquisition of nonverbal sign systems, or, to what extent are nonverbal signs language-mediated?

To specialists in many branches of industry, construction and assembly plans are clear without a verbal detour. To laymen, they must be explained. But they had to be explained to the specialist as well during his apprenticeship or studies! Here language is the medium for the acquisition process of nonverbal signs.

Mounin quoted mathematicians and logicians who are able to think consistently in their sign systems without recourse to language. I tend to believe in a rudimentary verbal procedure of which the person who is busy with arithmetical, operational, elimination, or abstraction processes all day long is no longer aware. The higher the level of reflection on which nonverbal signs are developed and used, the more this rudimentary procedure will be withdrawn from consciousness; the lower the level of reflection, the more easily this verbal aid will approach the rudimentary notion of the respective natural language which corresponds to the international sign, in the case of great weariness, nervous stress, or senility, and will be amplified to clearly perceptible mouth movements, to murmuring.

We will have to consider how signs and sign systems become independent, are technicalized and abstracted.[67] An aetiological study would be necessary here.

For Umberto Eco (1968/1972) two lines of semiological research stand out: (1) the claim for a synchronic examination of the various closed and strictly structured systems; (2) from the experience and perspective of a progressive semiosis (1968, p. 413), the notion of the communication model of an open process with variable codes and constant adaptation of the system.

Circumstances as an intentional element of communication (1972, p. 441) lead Eco to a revolutionary view of the pragmatic energy of the semiological conscience in the context of action systems (1972, p.441).

Habermas (1972/1973, p. 212) distinguished between norm and principle in the sense of a metanorm according to which norms may be produced. Forms of societies and nations, ideologies, branches of industrial production, and branches of science have developed conscious sign norms. How far we have approached sign principles, I would not risk to say, in spite of the extensive semiotic and semiological literature of recent years. When these principles are determined, we will have to clarify the sign-scientific relations for every field of art and practice, with their aid.[68]

We will especially have to consider how far signs and sign systems can be related to cognitive or normative models and how far they can be integrated into action theories as perspective presuppositions or as interactions.

5.5 SIGN COMPETENCE

We will have to discover how far the standardization of nonverbal signs may go, and at what point a remnant of unconscious behavior must remain as a token of humanity; to what degree sign competence should be supported and adopted in education programmes, which would have to be extended to the mass media.

Sign competence is closely connected with communicative competence. Each will partly include the other; I do not, however, want to equate them. Each of the competences proposed by Habermas (1972/1973, p. 195): language competence, cognitive competence, and role competence, covers part of general sign competence. But neither could sign competence be called the summary of the three competences proposed by Habermas, nor may the sum of these competences be considered communicative competence. Habermas (p. 196) assigned interaction norms to language competence. In our opinion, they should be extended to sign competence.

The acquisition of sign competence as an élite expert knowledge has been promoted most in art and film academies. That explains our relatively frequent reference to film theories. Fulchignoni (Rome) and Pasolini have already been mentioned. Work of great consequence has been done by Norman McLaren and the National Film Board of Canada. The dissection of sequences into drawn and painted single pictures for trick films demanded much more sign competence and abstract thinking in signs than acting in front of a camera in co-operation with the recording team.

5.6 THEORETIZATION

The theoretization of nonverbal signs on the one hand depends on language theory, on the other hand has to develop its own methods. Just like language theory, it has to be seen in interdisciplinary connexions. Just like language theory, it is now on the point of being absorbed into philosophical action theories.

We will have to beware of claiming to have established theories when we mention methods which are useful heuristically: classifications, the search for minimal units taken from structuralism, the application of psychological test results. We will have these theories only when we have done as much empirical and intellectual work with a pragmatic intention for a general sign science as has been done since Saussure for the synchronic examination of single languages and for the universal problem of human language.

Notes

[1] The 'application of sign theory to research in linguistic communication' is to be one of the main interests of the "Foundations of Communication" founded by Roland Posner (Berlin).
[2] Nonverbal signs are not mentioned at all by H. A. Gleason (1955/1961), *An Introduction to Descriptive Linguistics* (New York: Holt, Rinehart and Winston), and by J. Lyons (1968), *Introduction to Theoretical Linguistics* (Cambridge: Cambridge University Press). Zellig S. Harris (1951/1960), *Structural Linguistics* (Chicago/London: The University of Chicago Press), expressed his opinion on our problems in ten lines out of 375 pages. He stressed that he did not want to deal with the question of nonverbal utterances and gestural utterances, as they correspond neither to the phonology nor to the morphology of language description, in which he is completely right. But he admitted their importance for social interaction (p. 55).
[3] The points of view range from the extreme standpoint that only man as a rational animal was privileged to perform a gesture, for every gesture was charged with history and *noblesse* (Eugène Masure, (1953) *Le signe* (Lille), p. 5), to the acknowledgement of 'animal language' as a communication system of full value, which may be perceptible acoustically (blackbird's song, warning cries of crows) or motorically and optically (bees), but also applies to the olfactory sense and includes infra-red and ultra-violet rays. Cf. D. Burckhardt, W. Schleidt, H. Altner (1966), *Signale der Tierwelt* (München); R. A. Gardner, B. T. Gardner (1969), "Teaching Sign Language to a Chimpanzee", *Science* 165, pp. 664–72.
[4] John Lyons allowed a place for J. C. Marshall's article "The Biology of Communication in Man and Animals" (Lyons 1970, pp. 229–41), but dissociated himself in the preface: "Language is radically different from all known forms of animal communication" (p. 229).
[5] Lange-Seidl 1972/1973, p. 106.
[6] Crystal (1971, pp. 239–40) insisted on language as the most used and highest developed form of human communication and refused to give this name to animal communication systems: "The linguist considers language as a distinctively human phenomenon. He would also refrain from using the word . . . when . . . we say that a bond of communication exists between musicians, conductor and composer, so that all three 'speak the same language'. "On pp. 240–43, Crystal stressed everything that excludes language 'modali-

ties' or isolated nonverbal signs from being classified as language or even being designated as language.

[7] Cf. Crystal 1971, p. 240.

[8] Lange-Seidl (1977), "Idiolektkomponenten", Contribution to the XIIth International Congress of Linguists, Vienna 1977, Abstracts, p. 80.

[9] Corder 1973, p. 261.

[10] Martinet (1969/1973) mentioned prosody as far as it is an element of a certain language system; the article on "Prosody" by C. Hagège in the same manual saw voice timbre only in connection with the entire language, not affected by persons or situations. Bünting (1971) mentioned prosodic elements as a constituent of speech (pp. 62, 84) in four lines out of 190 pages.

[11] Laver/Hutcheson 1972, p. 12 (Introduction); Sapir 1927/1972; Birdwhistell 1961/1972.

[12] "Les lois que découvrira la sémiologie seront applicables à la linguistique. ... La tâche du linguiste est de définir ce qui fait de la langue un système spécial dans l'ensemble des faits sémiologiques" (Saussure 1916/1962, p. 3). This special system of language in the total sign system 'semiology', which characterizes Saussure's sign conception, is perverted by Roland Barthes 1970: "La linguistique n'est pas une partie, même priviligiée, de la science des signes, c'est la sémiologie qui est partie de la linguistique: Très précisément cette partie qui prendrait en charge les grandes unités signifiantes du discours" (p. 9). But it is not as if Roland Barthes understood linguistics better than nonverbal signs; *L'empire des signes* (1970) proves the contrary. The opinion "Le signe est une fracture qui ne s'ouvre que sur le visage d'un autre signe" also stems from Roland Barthes (1970, p. 66) and needs to be examined more closely.

[13] Peirce 1897/1960, p. 330.

[14] Cf. Bense 1967; Walther 1974 offers a detailed delineation of Peirce's sign theory.

[15] European readers are affronted by Morris' building up of his sign system with the vocabulary of Behaviorism. But even readers who consider Zipf's Law naive but intelligible, who take pleasure in examples from Skinner's *Verbal Behavior* and consider his essays on the control of human behavior excellent, consider the experiments with dogs and cats, which Morris did not carry out himself, hypothetical, and do not believe in his indirect evidence. Mounin (1970, p. 66) thinks there is much more of solid semiology in Saussure's fifteen fragmentary remarks than in Morris' numerous pages.

[16] The English collective notion 'semiotics' for a classified sign science was first used by Margaret Mead as meaning the "study of all patterned communication in all modalities", with stress on the cultural determination of behavior in communication processes.

[17] "La linguistique peut devenir le patron général de toute sémiologie, bien que la langue ne soit qu'un système particulier" (1916/1962, p. 101).

[18] Cf. Hjelmslev 1943/1966. Why Francis J. Whitfield in his English version (1969: *Prolegomena to a Theory of Language*) translated *sprog* with 'semiotic' in paragraphs clearly related to language, is obscure. *Konnotationssprog og metasprog* in Chapter 22 was translated 'connotative semiotics'. In Chapter 21 Hjelmslev defined language (*sprog*) as a hierarchy; Whitfield defined 'semiotic' as a hierarchy. Garroni was a victim of this conscious or unconscious misinterpretation. He based two books on it, as he had access only to the English and the Italian version, but not to the original. He, for his part, accused the Italian version of inexact translation. The Italian version refers to the original. We must insert 'language' where Whitfield used 'semiotic', thus p. 96: where lies the border between 'language and non-language (verbal and nonverbal)' instead of 'semiotic and non-semiotic'. Where Hjelmslev distinguished between colloquial speech and text, Whitfield translated 'language' and text, which did not meet Hjelmslev's intentions. Mathematical sign language is translated 'mathematical semiotic' by Whitfield which yields little sense. To translate individual language with 'individual semiotic' is deliberately misleading. Language structure became 'linguistic scheme' with Whitfield; in the paragraph on metalanguage, the translation of *sprog* as 'semiotic' is especially troublesome. What Hjelmslev actually wrote on metasemiology thereby completely lost its value.

[19] Lange-Seidl 1972/1973, p. 108.
[20] The ten different codes which Umberto Eco discerned for film show the lines which could be taken as a basis for theoretization of nonverbal signs: psychology, anthropology, information theory, communication models, connotations and conventions are referred to. Cf. 1968/1972, pp. 20–27.
[21] "It is necessary that a generative grammar have ... a semantic or message component, and also a pragmatic or, more generally, a medium component."
[22] B. Schlieben-Lange (1973), *Soziolinguistik: Eine Einführung* (Stuttgart), p. 73.
[23] Cf. Vernon 1966/1970; Haber 1968, 1969.
[24] The author hopes to be able to present the results of a study on the releasing factors which cause the transition between different degrees of perception within the verbal range. A contribution "De la perception à la conception des signes" was presented at the Colloquium "Langage et Pensée Mathématiques", Luxemburg, June 1976.
[25] Cf. Osgood/Miron 1963, p. 132.
[26] Roland Barthes considered photography a message without code, but containing so many connotations that their totality would make up a kind of rhetoric for photography.
[27] Corresponding to John L. Austin (1962), *How to Do Things with Words*, an essay "How to Do Things with Signs" should be written; especially the intersections between action by speech and action by nonverbal signs should be closely investigated.
[28] If Julia Kristeva (1967, p. 29) wanted to define semiotics as the production of models, as a point of intersection of sciences in a theoretical process, and preferred to use 'semiotic level' instead of 'semiotics', a level of axiomatization for formalizing sign systems, the question arises whether she placed these claims on the object level or metalevel. In another passage (1967, p. 27) she advocated the opinion that all actions could be investigated scientifically as a system of relations to natural language, as social practice nowadays is considered a structured system like a language. She did not attach language to action theories as pragmatics does, but instead attached action to language theories.
[29] In this way the title *Semiotic Approaches to Psychiatry* by Harley C. Shands (1970, Den Haag: Mouton) is to be understood, a title which, in a semiotic series (*Approaches to Semiotics*, ed. Thomas A. Sebeok, vol. 2) is deceptive at first sight, as only the symptoms of psychiatry are presented, but not conscious sign giving.
[30] Cf. Stokoe 1960 and 1972, where the gestures which American deaf-mutes use are commented on; cf. also Stokoe/Croneberg/Casterline (1965), a clearly arranged dictionary with drawings for the American deaf-mute 'sign language'. Furth's studies on the deaf-mute problem by far exceed the descriptive phase of semiotics. According to Piaget, Furth (1966) approached a great many problems which arise in connection with a theoretization in the nonverbal domain.
[31] Guilhot (1963) offered such a description, which could be used as a basis for semiotic research.
[32] Heat radiations of the human body are symptoms which may function as stimuli on other persons and thereby may provoke a movement towards another body or away from another body (Hall 1963, p. 1014).
[33] American proxemic researchers are therefore extremely sensitive to olfactory impression in other countries. Cf. Hall 1963, p. 1015; Diebold 1968, p. 537.
[34] Cf. Shands 1970; on the basis of behaviorism, Watzlawick/Beavin/Jackson 1967 examine sign processes, especially in connection with the "Double Bind Theory".
[35] Cf. Goffman 1961/1973.
[36] "On peut concevoir une science qui étudie la vie des signes au sein de la vie sociale: elle formerait une partie de la psychologie sociale; nous la nommerons sémiologie.... C'est au psychologue à déterminer la place exacte de la sémiologie" (Saussure 1916/1962, p. 3).
[37] "Gestalt theory had the merit of introducing ... the idea that certain perceptual

structures can impel changes to restore 'equilibrium' "(D. E. Berlyne, "Experimental aesthetics", in: P. C. Dodwell, ed. (1972), *New Horizons in Psychology* 2 (Harmondsworth: Penguin), p. 114).

[38] Karl Bühler (1960) gave a résumé of shape theories and their possible consequences. He put the expressiveness of the human face into the centre of his considerations. Cf. also K. Koffka (1922/1970), "Perception: An Introduction to Gestalt-Theorie", in: Vernon, ed., 1966/1970, pp. 17–32, as well as in the other articles in this reader; cf. Lange-Seidl 1976a and 1976b.

[39] Some people need eye contact, proximity, in order to perceive every twitch of their partners' muscles as an expression of emotion; others want distance in order to have a general view of body contour, the interaction of the body movements in front of their eyes. Some persons shut their eyes while speaking or do not look directly at their partners, which may lead to less interaction, but also to a more relevant use of acoustic signs. Howard/Templeton (1966, p. 13) consider the 'retinal image' which arises in the eye of the sign perceiver as a 'proximal stimulus'. This behavioristic interpretation is certainly too narrow here. We should rather assume an interplay between the natural form of vision and cultural indoctrination. Thus, flat two-dimensional vision may be a natural predisposition; but it is supported by painting and drawings without backgrounds. Persons who see only contours, not bodies, are able to make those shadow-like mental images an aesthetic obligation for others and thereby establish them culturally. This is a reciprocal process: culture comes to meet the expectations, intensifies those natural visual tendencies and makes them conventional.

[40] At the Interdisciplinary Symposium on the Philosophy of Science and Linguistics, Salzburg, Jan. 1974, Gerhard Frey called analyses of reflection the most important approach to the pragmatic aspects of linguistics. He extended this claim to nonverbal signs. Cf. Frey (1966), "Reflexionsanalysen von Texten", *Studium Generale* 19, Heft 7. Two articles by Frey, "Begrenzungsfunktion des Bewußtseins" and "Formalstruktur und natürliche Sprache", contain thoughts on reflection processes and levels of consciousness which should be considered for nonverbal signs too.

[41] Cf. Furth 1969/1972, especially the bibliography of Piaget's publications in the German version and the preface by Piaget himself, in which he assumed an infinite series of reflexive abstractions and a central factor of equilibrium, which was indispensable for the explanation of development. Cf. also Habermas 1970/1973, p. 273, on the functional circle of instrumental action.

[42] Furth 1969/1972. The difference between the signal, which Furth attaches to Behaviorism, and the symbol (p. 44) has not been stressed sharply enough. The distinction between intelligent and logical thought is important (p. 230).

[43] Furth 1969/1972; cf. the keyword 'representative'.

[44] Furth 1969/1972, p. 60, and the keyword 'equilibration'.

[45] Habermas 1970/1973, p. 274.

[46] Klaus 1963, p. 61. According to him, behavioristic sign theory was applicable to traffic signs and musical notes. That was probably reflected too hastily. As regards traffic signs, I may ignore them at any time if I take the consequences. Thus they are not an immediate stimulus for the pedestrian. As the punishment is much heavier for car-drivers than for pedestrians or cyclists, the procedure becomes automatized in them. As a pedestrian, I can stand at a traffic light for hours and watch the traffic, or simply talk to a friend, without experiencing the red light as a stimulus for myself every time. Stimulus and response would only be present if I crossed the street every time at the green light for pedestrians and returned during the next green phase. As a reflecting human being, I may stand there and think about the density of the traffic, makes of car or other phenomena. Even if I am waiting for a person or bus, the traffic light is not a stimulus for me. Musical notation is certainly no stimulus: without realization, it does not lead to any behavior. Musical notation on the paper has not

yet moved a dancer's leg. It is in situation zero. Only the human subject is able to make it effective, in a process which is composed of conscious elements known by training, and unconscious ones known by musicality.

[47] Cf. Lange-Seidl 1974. Signs with zero value, signs in zero situation, non-existent signs, sign substitution, zero-status of sign and subject are distinguished.

[48] Cf. Resnikow's sign definition, p. 14, and his signal definition, p. 143.

[49] A. D. Ritchie (1936), *The Natural History of Mind* (London/New York: Longmans, Green and Co.), p. 278.

[50] E. Cassirer (1923–1929), *Philosophie der symbolischen Formen* (Berlin: B. Cassirer).

[51] The logical and the psychological aspects are combined in the English concept 'meaning' and their reciprocal effect produces a debatable multiplicity for the relations of significances.

[52] For example, the phases of traffic lights are regulated according to time, but this time interval corresponds to the frequency of the traffic at certain crossings, that means it depends on space. In the desert or in a park, a traffic light temporarily switching from red to green would be absurd. Therefore it could play a symbolic role for 'empty meaning' in a satirical play or film.

[53] In his musicological publications, Stockhausen demands the conscious inclusion of space and time in music, as in Baroque music, which still worked with echo effects in time sequence according to the premises of spatial distance when Lessing wrote his 'Laokoon'.

[54] According to Lanigan (1972, p. 140), Merleau-Ponty rejected spatiality for film. He used film as a paradigm of time shape, as everything was time-person relation in film. According to this, proxemic laws would not be valid for film, the distinctness of mime and gesture would be meaningless, the efforts of the camera team at correct focusing absurd, if only chronological order were considered. Maybe Merleau-Ponty was talking about amateur silent films.

[55] Cf. also Krampen 1973.

[56] These ideas are argued in detail by Walther 1974.

[57] Cf. Robinson 1972, pp. 38–56, especially the scheme on p. 44, which includes nonverbal signs too.

[58] Alexandre 1969 dealt with tambourine languages in Africa, which lost their function as telecommunication systems with the introduction of writing and modern mass media (p. 274); cf. Lange-Seidl 1976b.

[59] If the intensity of the voice follows cultural norms and is to be valued as a significant variable for the estimation of distances, the other two variables dependent on each other, relation between partners and situation, would have to be kept neutral. Conversely, distance and situation may be neutralized themselves in order to infer the relation, or situation may be isolated if distance and relation are neutralized (Hall 1963, p. 1016).

[60] While an American makes himself comfortable with his feet on an office desk between him and his partner, a Chinese has a feeling of being examined if a table separates him from his interlocutor (Hall 1963, p. 1006).

[61] Mounin sees one difficulty in the Americans calling 'symbol' what European semiologists call *signe* or *Zeichen*.

[62] Robinson (1972, pp. 113–14) called our attention to video-recording experiments carried out by Argyle 1970. The persons questioned valued nonverbal cues four times higher than verbal ones, which could only operate as multipliers. In other test series, the nonverbal cues were even six times more influential. If nonverbal and verbal cues were in conflict, the test persons judged a speaker insincere if the verbal cues were friendly, the nonverbal ones hostile, but were only confused if the verbal cues were hostile but the nonverbal ones friendly. Obviously these tests show that we consider it more difficult to control face and voice than to programme the contents of a verbal utterance.

[63] Cf. Fulchignoni 1969, especially the chapters on degrees of reality and presence of pictures in film.

[64] Of great interest is Sebeok's attempt to classify according to sources, recipients, and channels of transmission. We must beware of confusing information processes, where nonverbal signs support the principle of negentropy, with tertiary electronic systems which transfer natural language into artificial programming languages.

[65] Cf. Rossi-Landi 1972.

[66] Numbers are more relevant than words: a single wrong number in an automatic telephone system connects us with strangers, while a wrong word, or still more a single wrong phoneme or grapheme, may be rendered ineffective by a redundant context.

[67] The policeman who directed the traffic by gestures was replaced by color signals, the time intervals of which are pre-controlled and the arrangement of which is clear to the color-blind as well.

References

Abercrombie, D.
  1968/1972 "Paralanguage", in: Laver/Hutcheson 1972, pp. 64–70.
Adams, P., ed.,
  1972 *Language in Thinking*. Harmondsworth: Penguin.
Alexandre, P.,
  1969 "Langages tambourinés: une écriture sonore?", *Semiotica* 1, pp. 273–81.
Argyle, M.,
  1967/1973 *The Psychology of Interpersonal Behaviour*. Harmondsworth: Penguin.
  1969 *Social Interaction*. Chicago: Methuan.
  1972 "Non-Verbal Communication in Human Social Interaction", in: Hinde 1972, pp. 243–69.
  1975 *Bodily Communication*. London: Methuan.
Austin, J. L.
  1962 *How to Do Things with Words*. Oxford: Oxford University Press.
Barre, W. La,
  1947/1972 "The Cultural Basis of Emotions and Gestures", in: Laver/Hutcheson 1972, pp. 207–24.
  1964 "Paralinguistics, Kinetics, and Cultural Anthropology", in: Sebeok/Hayes/Bateson 1964, pp. 191–237.
  1972 "Ethology and Ethnology", *Semiotica* 6, pp. 83–96.
Barthes, R.,
  1970 *L'empire des signes*. Genf: Skira.
Bateson, G.,
  1968 "Redundancy and Coding", in: Sebeok 1968, pp. 614–26.
Baudrillard, J.,
  1972 *Pour une critique de l'économie politique du signe*. Paris: Gallimard.
Bense, M.,
  1967 *Semiotik: Allgemeine Theorie der Zeichen*. Baden-Baden: Agis.
  1969 *Einführung in die informationstheoretische Ästhetik*. Reinbek bei Hamburg: Rowohlt.
  1975 *Semiotische Prozesse und Systeme*. Baden-Baden: Agis.
Bense, M., und E. Walther, eds.,
  1973 *Wörterbuch der Semiotik*. Köln: Kiepenheuer und Witsch.

Bertalanffy, L. v.,
1971 "General Theory of Systems: Application to Psychology", in: Kristeva/Rey-Debove/Umiker 1971, pp. 191–203.
Bettetini, G.,
1973 *The Language and Technique of the Film.* The Hague: Mouton.
Birdwhistell, R. L.,
1952 *Introduction to Kinesics.* Louisville: University of Louisville Press.
1961/1972 "Paralanguage Twenty-Five Years after Sapir", in: Laver/Hutcheson 1972, pp. 82–100.
1970 *Kinesics and Context.* Philadelphia: University of Pennsylvania Press.
Bolzano, B.,
1837 *Wissenschaftslehre.* Sulzbach: Seidel [Cf. also Walther 1971].
Bouissac, P.,
1973 *La mesure des gestes: Prolégomènes à la sémiotique gestuelle.* The Hague: Mouton.
Brekle, H.,
1972 *Semantik.* München: Fink.
Bühler, K.,
1933 *Ausdruckstheorie.* Jena: Fischer.
1960 *Das Gestaltprinzip im Leben der Menschen und der Tiere.* Bern/Stuttgart: H. Huber.
Bünting, K.-D.
1971 *Einführung in die Linguistik.* Frankfurt: Athenäum.
Canter, D. V., ed.,
1969 *Architectural Psychology,* Proceedings of the Conference Held at Dalandhui, University of Strathclyde.
Cherry, C.,
1957 *On Human Communication,* Cambridge, Mass: MIT-Press.
Cicourel, A. V.,
1973 *Cognitive Sociology; Language and Meaning in Social Interaction.* Harmondsworth: Penguin.
Corder, S. P.,
1973 *Introducing Applied Linguistics.* Harmondsworth: Penguin.
Coseriu, E.,
1967 "L'arbitraire du signe: Zur Spätgeschichte eines aristotelischen Begriffes", *Archiv für das Stadium der Neueren Sprachen und Literaturen,* 204, pp. 81–112.
Crystal, D.,
1971 *Linguistics.* Harmondsworth: Penguin.
1974 "Paralinguistics", in: Sebeok 1974, pp. 265–97.
Crystal, D., and R. Quirk,
1964 *Systems of Prosodic and Paralinguistic Features in English.* The Hague: Mouton.
Diebold, A. R.,
1968 "Anthropological Perspectives", in: Sebeok 1968, pp. 525–571.
Eco, U.,
1968 *La struttura assente.* Milano: Bompiani. [German version by J. Trabant, 1972: *Einführung in die Semiotik,* München: Fink/UTB.]
1968 "Die Gliederung des filmischen Code", *Sprache im technischen Zeitalter,* 27, pp. 230–252. [1971 in: Knilli 1971, pp. 70–93.]
1971 *Le forme del contenuto.* Milano: Bompiani.
1972 "Introduction to a Semiotics of Iconic Signs", *Versus* 2, pp. 1–16.
1973 *Il segno.* Milano: ISEDI.
1975a *A Theory of Semiotics,* Bloomington/London: Indiana University Press.
1975b *Trattato di semiotica generale,* Milano: Bompiani
Efron, D.,
1941 *Gesture and Environment,* New York: King's Crown Press. [1971 The Hague: Mouton.]

Ekman, P., ed.,
   1973 *Darwin and Facial Expression: A Century of Research in Review*. New York: Academic Press.
Ekman, P. and W. V. Friesen,
   1969 "The Repertoire of Nonverbal Behavior: Categories, Origins, Usage, and Coding", *Semiotica* 1, pp. 49-98.
   1972 "Hand Movements", *The Journal of Communication* 22, pp. 353-74.
   1975 *Unmasking the Face*. Englewood Cliffs: Prentice Hall.
Ekman, P., W. V. Friesen, P. Ellesworth,
   1972 *Emotion in the Human Face: Guidelines for Research and an Integration of Findings*, New York: Pergamon Press.
Eschbach, A.,
   1974 *Zeichen, Text, Bedeutung: Bibliographie zu Theorie und Praxis der Semiotik*, München: Fink.
Eschbach, A., und W. Rader
   1976 *Semiotik-Bibliographie* I. Frankfurt: Syndikat.
Farrell, B.A.,
   1954-1955 "Intentionality and the Theory of Signs", *Philosophy and Phenomenological Research* 15, pp. 500-11.
Fulchignoni, E.,
   1969 *La civilisation de l'image*. Paris: Payot.
Furth, H. G.,
   1966 *Thinking without Language*. New York: Free Press/London: Collier-Macmillan.
   1969 *Piaget and Knowledge: Theoretical Foundations*. Englewood Cliffs: Prentice Hall.
Goffman, E.,
   1959 *The Presentation of Self in Everyday Life*. New York: Doubleday.
   1963 *Behavior in Public Places*. New York: Free Press.
Goldman-Eisler, F.,
   1968 *Psycholinguistics: Experiments in Spontaneous Speech*, London/New York: Academic Press.
Greenlee, Douglas,
   1973 *Peirce's Concept of Sign*. The Hague: Mouton.
Greimas, A. J., ed.,
   1970 *Sign, Language, Culture*. The Hague: Mouton.
Guilhot, J.,
   1962 *De la dynamique de l'expression et de la communication: La voix, la parole, les mimiques et gestes auxiliaires*. The Hague: Mouton.
Guiraud, P.,
   1971 *La sémiologie*, Paris: Presses Universitaires.
Gumperz, J., and D. Hymes, eds.,
   1964 "The Ethnography of Communication", *American Anthropologist* 66/6, 2.
Haber, R. N., ed.,
   1968 *Contemporary Theory and Research in Visual Perception*. New York: Holt, Rinehart and Winston.
   1969 *Information-Processing Approaches to Visual Perception*, New York: Holt, Rinehart and Winston.
Habermas, J.,
   1970/1973 "Der Universalitätsanspruch der Hermeneutik", in: Habermas 1973, pp. 264-301.
   1971a "Vorbereitende Bemerkungen zu einer Theorie der kommunikativen Kompetenz", in: Habermas/Luhmann 1971, pp. 101-41.
   1971b "Meaning of Meaning, oder: Ist Sinn eine sprachunabhängige Kategorie?", in: Habermas/Luhmann 1971, pp. 171-202.
   1972/1973 "Notizen zum Begriff der Rollenkompetenz", in: Habermas 1973, pp. 195-231.

1973 *Kultur und Kritik,* Frankfurt: Suhrkamp.
Habermas, J., und N. Luhmann,
    1971 *Theorie der Gesellschaft,* Frankfurt: Suhrkamp.
Hall, E. T.,
    1969 *The Silent Language,* New York: Doubleday.
    1963 "A System for the Notation of Proxemic Behavior", in: Laver/Hutcheson 1972, pp. 247–73.
    1964 "Adumbration as a Feature of Intercultural Communication", *American Anthropologist* 66, pp. 154–63.
    1966/1969 *The Hidden Dimension* New York: Doubleday, [1969 London/Sydney/Toronto: The Bodley Head.]
    1968 "Proxemics", *Current Anthropology* 9, pp. 83–108.
Harrison, R. P.,
    1974 "Nonverbal Communication", in: I. de S. Pohl. and W. Schramm eds., *Handbook of Communication,* pp. 93–115.
Hinde, R. A., ed.,
    1972 *Non-verbal Communication,* Cambridge: Cambridge University Press.
Hjelmslev, L.,
    1943/1966 *Omkring Sprogteoriens Grundlaeggelse.* København: Akad. Forlag.
Höllerer, Walther,
    1974 "Welt aus Sprache zum Beispiel", *Sprache im technischen Zeitalter* 50, pp. 175–84; [English version 1975: "World of Language as Example", *Versus* 10/4, pp. 78–85.]
Houston, S. H.,
    1972 *A Survey of Psycholinguistics,* The Hague: Mouton.
Howard, J. P., and W. B. Templeton,
    1966 *Human Spatial Orientation,* London/New York/Sydney: Wiley.
Hymes, D. H.,
    1971 "On Communicative Competence", in: J. B. Pride, and J. Holmes, eds., *Sociolinguistics,* pp. 269–293. Harmondsworth: Penguin.
Jakobson, R.,
    1974 "Coup d'oeil sur le développement de la sémiotique", *Actes du Premier Congrès de l'Association Internationale de Sémiotique, Milan.* The Hague: Mouton (in print).
Kamlah, W., and P. Lorenzen
    1967 *Logische Propädeutik.* Mannheim: Bibliographisches Institut.
Kelley, D. L.,
    1971 *Kinesiology: Fundamentals of Motion Description,* Englewood Cliffs: Prentice Hall.
Kendon, A., R. M. Harris, *et al.,* eds.,
    1975 *Organization of Behavior in Face-to-Face Interaction.* The Hague: Mouton.
Klaus, G.,
    1963 *Semiotik und Erkenntnistheorie,* Berlin: Deutscher Verlag d. Wiss. [1973 München/Salzburg: Fink.]
Knapp, M. L.,
    1972 *Non-verbal Communication in Human Interaction,* New York: Holt, Rinehart and Winston.
Knilli, F.,
    1968 "Präliminarien zur Kinosemiologie", *Sprache im technischen Zeitalter,* 27, pp. 181–84.
Knilli, F., ed.,
    1971 *Semiotik des Films.* München: Hanser.
Krames, L., *et al.,*
    1974 *Nonverbal Communication,* New York/London: Plenum Press.

Krampen, M.,
 1973 "Iconic Signs, Supersigns and Models", *Versus* 4, pp. 101–108.
Kristeva, J.,
 1967 "L'expansion de le sémiotique", *Information sur les Sciences Sociales* 6/5, pp. 169–81.
 1969 *Semeiotike; Recherches pour une sémanalyse,* Paris, Seuil.
Kristeva, J., J., Rey-Debove, D. J. Umiker, eds.,
 1971 *Essays in Semiotics.* The Hague: Mouton.
Lange-Seidl, A.,
 1972/1973 "Psycholinguistik", *Dillingen-Report* 13, pp. 78–109. Dillingen/Donau.
 1974 "Signe du zéro, zéro de signe", *Actes du Premier Congrès de l'Association Internationale de Sémiotique, Milan.* The Hague: Mouton (in print).
 1975a "Ansatzpunkte für Theorien nichtverbaler Zeichen", in: Schlieben-Lange 1975a.
 1975b "Semiotics versus Semiology: Towards a General Sign Theory", in: *International Congress of Logic, Methodology and Philosophy of Science, London/Ontario, Contributed Papers* XI, pp. 11–12.
 1976a "Transferierbare Zeichensysteme und das Wesen der Kunst", *Acta Germanica* 9, pp. 1–7. Cape Town.
 1976b "Grenzen der Austauschbarkeit von Zeichensystemen", *Akten des II. Wiener Symposiums über Semiotik,* München: Fink (in print).
 1976c "De la perception à la conception des signes", *Actes du Colloque International 'Langage et pensèe mathématiques',* Luxemburg (in print).
Langer, S. K.,
 1942 *Philosophy in a New Key.* Cambridge, Mass.: Harvard University Press.
 1953 *Feeling and Form: A Theory of Art.* New York/London: Scribner's Sons.
Lanigan, R. L.,
 1972 *Speaking and Semiology: Maurice Merleau-Ponty's Phenomenological Theory of Existential Communication.* The Hague: Mouton.
Laver, J., and S. Hutcheson, eds.,
 1972 *Communication in Face to Face Interaction.* Harmondsworth: Penguin.
Lindekens, R.,
 1971 *Eléments pour une sémiotique de la photographie,* Bruxelles: AIMAV/Paris: Didier.
Locke, J.,
 1690 *Essay Concerning Humane Understanding.* London: Thomas Basset.
Luhmann, N.,
 1971 "Sinn als Grundbegriff der Soziologie", in: Habermas/Luhmann 1971, pp: 25–100.
Lyons, J., ed.,
 1970 *New Horizons in Linguistics.* Harmondsworth: Penguin
Madsen, P.,
 1971 *Semiotik og Dialektik.* København: Munksgaard.
Martinet, A.,
 1960 *Eléments de linguistique générale.* Paris: Colin.
 1965 *La linguistique synchronique.* Paris: Presses Universitaires.
Martinet, A., ed.,
 1969/1973 *Linguistik: Ein Handbuch.* Stuttgart: Metzlersche Verlagsbuchhandlung.
Martinet, J.,
 1973 *Clefs pour la sémiologie.* Paris: Seghers.
Melbin, M.,
 1974 "Some Issues in Nonverbal Communication", *Semiotica* 10, pp. 293–304.
Metz, Ch.,
 1971 *Langage et cinéma.* Paris: Larousse. [German version by M. Theume/A. Ros,

1973 *Sprache und Film*, Frankfurt: Athenäum: [English version by D. J. Umiker-Sebeok, 1974: *Language and Cinema*, The Hague: Mouton.]

Moles, A.,
  1958 *Théorie de l'information et perception esthétique.* Paris: Flammarion [German version by H. Ronge, 1971: *Informationstheorie und ästhetische Wahrnehmung.* Köln: DuMont Schauberg.]
  1967 *Sociodynamique de la culture,* The Hague: Mouton.

Morris, Ch.,
  1938 *Foundations of the Theory of Signs,* Chicago: University of Chicago Press; [German version 1972: *Grundlagen der Zeichentheorie,* München: Hanser.]
  1946 *Signs, Language, and Behavior.* New York: Prentice Hall.
  1964 *Signification and Significance,* Cambridge, Mass.: MIT Press.
  1971 *Writings on the General Theory of Signs,* The Hague: Mouton.
  1977 *Pragmatische Semiotik und Handlungstheorie,* German version, ed. by A. Eschbach. Frankfurt: Suhrkamp.

Mounin, G.,
  1970 *Introduction à la sémiologie.* Paris: Minuit.

Osgood, Ch., and M. S. Miron., eds.,
  1963 *Approaches to the Study of Aphasia: A Report of an Interdisciplinary Conference on Aphasia.* Urbana: University of Illinois Press.

Parret, Herman,
  1975 *Idéologie et sémiologie chez Locke et Condillac: La question de l'autonomie du langage devant la pensée.* Lisse: Peter de Ridder Press.

Pasolini, P. P.,
  1966 "Die Sprache des Films", *Film 2,* pp. 49; [in: Knilli 1971, pp. 38–55.]

Peirce, Ch. S.,
  1965–66 *Collected Papers of Charles Sanders Peirce,* ed. by Ch. Hartshorne et al., 6 vols. Cambridge, Mass.: Harvard University Press.
  1906 "Prolegomena to an Apology for Pragmatism", *The Monist,* pp. 492–546.

Peuser, G., ed.
  1976 *Interdisziplinäre Aspekte der Aphasieforschung: Festschrift für Anton Leischner.* Köln: Rheinland-Verlag.

Piaget, J.,
  1970 *Epistémologie des sciences de l'homme.* Paris: Gallimard.

Popper, F.,
  1967 *Naissance de l'art cinétique.* Paris: Gauthier-Villard.

Prieto, L. L.,
  1966a *La sémiologie* (= *Encyclopédie de la Pléiade,* vol. *Langage*). Paris.
  1966b *Messages et signaux,* Paris: Presses Universitaires [German version by G. Wotjak, 1972: *Nachrichten und Signale,* Berlin: Akademie-Verlag/München: Hueber.]
  1975a *Pertinence et pratique.* Paris: Minuit.
  1975b *Etudes de linguistique et de sémiologie générale.* Paris: Droz.

Raffler-Engel, W. V.,
  1975 *Cultural Differences in Kinesics.* Nashville.

Ramat, Paolo,
  1975 "Semiotics and Linguistics", *Versus* 10/1, pp. 1–16.

Resnikow, L. O.,
  1964 [German version 1968: *Erkenntnistheoretische Fragen der Semiotik.* Berlin: Akademie-Verlag.]

Rey, A.,
  1973 *Théories du signe et du sens,* Paris: Klincksieck.

Robinson, W. P.,
  1972 *Language and Social Behaviour,* Harmondsworth: Penguin.

Rossi-Landi, F.,
   1972 *Semiotica e ideologia*. Milano: Bompiani.
Ruesch, J.,
   1972 *Semiotic Approaches to Human Relations*. The Hague: Mouton.
Ruesch, Y, and W. Kees.,
   1956 *Nonverbal Communication*, Berkeley/Los Angeles: University of California Press.
Sampson, G.,
   1972 "Natural Language and the Paradox of the Liar", *Semiotica* 5, pp. 305–23.
Saussure, F. de,
   1916/1962⁵ *Cours de Linguistique générale*. Paris: Payot.
Schaeffer, P.,
   1966 *Traité des objets musicaux*, Paris: Seuil.
Schlieben-Lange, B.
   1975 "Metasprache und Metakommunikation", in: Schlieben-Lange, ed., 1975, pp. 189–205.
   1975 *Linguistische Pragmatik*, Stuttgart: Kohlhammer.
Schlieben-Lange, B., ed.
   1975 *Sprachtheorie*, Hamburg: Hoffmann und Campe.
Searle, J. R.,
   1969 *Speech acts*, Cambridge: Cambridge University Press, [German version by R. and R. Wiggershaus, 1971 *Sprechakte*, Frankfurt: Suhrkamp.]
   1975b "Sei specie de segni: proposte e critiche", *Versus* 11, 1, pp. 1–27.
Sebeok, Th. A.
   1974 "Nonverbal Communication", *Actes du Premier Congrès de l'Association Internationale de Sémiotique, Milan*. The Hague: Mouton (in print).
Sebeok, Th. A., ed.
   1968 *Animal Communication*. Bloomington: Indiana University Press.
   1969 *Semiotica: Journal of the International Association for Semiotic Studies*.
   1974 *Current Trends in Linguistics* 12. The Hague: Mouton.
   1975 *The Tell-Tale Sign: A Survey of Semiotics*. Lisse: Peter de Ridder Press.
Sebeok, The A., A. S. Hayes, and M. C. Bateson, eds.
   1964 *Approaches to Semiotics*. The Hague: Mouton.
Shands, H. C.,
   1970 *Semiotic Approaches to Psychiatry*. The Hague: Mouton.
Stokoe, W. C.,
   1960 *Sign Language Structure: An Outline of the Visual Communication Systems of the American Deaf* (= Studies in Linguistics 8).
   1974 "Motor Signs as the First Form of Language", *Semiotica* 10, pp. 117–30.
   1975 "Face-to-Face Interaction: Signs to Language", in Kendon/Harris 1975, pp. 315–37.
Stokoe, W. C., C. Croneberg, D. Casterline,
   1965 *A Dictionary of American Sign Language*, Washington, D. C.: Gallaudet College Press.
Trabant, J.,
   1970 *Zur Semiologie des literarischen Kunstwerks*. München: Fink.
   1975 "Vom Sinn", in: Schlieben-Lange, ed., 1975, pp. 277–85.
   1976 *Elemente der Semiotik*, München: Beck.
Trager, G. L.,
   1958 "Paralanguage; A First Approximation", *Studies in Linguistics* 13, pp. 1–12.
Vernon, M. D., ed.,
   1966/1970: *Experiments in Visual Perception*, Harmondsworth: Penguin.
Verón, E.,
   1973 "Pour une sémiologie des opérations translinguistiques", *Versus* 4, pp. 81–100.

Walther, E.,
1974 *Allgmeine Zeichenlehre,* Stuttgart: Deutsche Verlagsanstalt.
Walther, E., ed.,
1971 *Bernard Bolzano, Semiotik* (= *rot* 43). Stuttgart: E. Walther.
Watson, O. M.,
1970 *Proxemic Behavior: A Cross-Cultural Study.* The Hague: Mouton.
Watson, D. M., and T. D. Graves,
1966 "Quantitative Research in Proxemic Behavior," *American Anthropologist* 68, pp. 971–85.
Watzlawick, P., J. Beavin, D. D., Jackson,
1967 *The Pragmatics of Human Communication*, New York: Norton.
Weitz, S., ed.,
1974 *Nonverbal Communication: Readings with Commentary.* New York: Oxford University Press.
Weydt, H.,
1975 "Mehrfachverständnis sprachlicher und nichtsprachlicher Zeichen", in: Drachman, G., ed., 1975: *Salzburger Beiträge zur Linguistik* I, pp. 239–54. Tübingen: Gunter Narr.
Wollen, P.,
1969 *Signs and Meaning in the Cinema.* London: Secker and Warburg.
Worth, S.,
1969 "The Development of a Semiotic of Film", *Semiotica* 1, pp. 282–321.
Wunderlich, D.,
1971 "Der kinetische Film", in: Knilli 1971, pp. 158–75.
Wundt, W.,
1921/1973 *The Language of Gestures.* The Hague: Mouton.

Index of Names

Alexandre, P. 33, 47
Altner, H. 43
Argyle, M. 47
Austin, J. L. 45

Barthes, R. 44–45
Bateson, G. 36
Baudrillard, J. 34
Beavin, J. 45
Bense, M. 14, 33, 44
Berlyne, D. E. 46
Bertalanffy, L. von 30
Bettetini, G. 19
Birdwhistell, R. L. 12, 16, 44
Birkhoff, G. D. 33
Bolzano, B. 13, 14
Bouissac, P. 38
Braille, L. 27
Bühler, K. 29, 36, 46
Bünting, K.-D. 44
Burckhardt, D. 43

Carnap, R. 31
Cassirer, E. 31, 47
Casterline, D. 45
Chomsky, N. 21
Corder, S. P. 44
Coseriu, E. 22
Croneberg, C. 45
Crystal, D. 43–44

Diebold, A. R. 29, 45
Dodwell, P. C. 46

Eco, U. 20, 24, 40, 45
Efron, D. 17
Einstein, A. 29, 32
Eschbach, A. 13

Flydal, L. 22
Frey, G. 46
Fulchignoni, E. 41, 48
Furth, H. G. 30, 38, 45–46

Gardner, B. T. 43
Gardner, R. A. 43
Garroni, E. 44
Gleason, H. A. 43
Goffman, E. 34, 45
Goldman-Eisler, F. 16
Guilhot, J. 45

Haber, R. N. 45
Habermas, J. 30, 35, 40–41, 46
Hagège, C. 44
Hall, E. T. 17, 28–29, 34, 38, 45, 47
Harris, Z. S. 43
Heidegger, M. 31
Hjelmslev, L. 15, 44
Houston, S. H. 21–22
Howard, J. P. 46
Husserl, E. 31
Hutcheson, S. 44

Jackson, D. D. 45
Jacoby, G. 29, 32

Jakobson, R. 9
Jaspers, K. 31

Kamlah, W. 31
Klaus, G. 30–31, 46
Koffka, K. 46
Krampen, M. 47
Kristeva, J. 45

Lange-Seidl, A. 12, 23, 25, 43–47
Langer, S. K. 31–32
Lanigan, R. L. 31, 47
Laver, J. 44
Lessing, G. E. 32
Lindekens, R. 18, 23
Locke, J. 13–14
Lorenzen, P. 30–31
Lyons, J. 43

Marcus, S. 9
Marshall, J. C. 43
Martinet, A. 16, 19, 44
Masure, E. 43
McLaren, N. 41
Mead, M. 34, 44
Melbin, M. 37
Merleau-Ponty, M. 31, 47
Metz, Chr. 18–20
Miron, M. S. 45
Morris, Ch. 14, 31, 44
Mounin, G. 25, 39–40, 44, 47

Ogden, C. K. 31
Osgood, Ch. 45

Pasolini, P. P. 19, 41
Peirce, Ch. S. 14, 31, 33, 44
Piaget, J. 30, 45–46

Popper, F. 16
Posner, R. 43
Prieto, L. 15

Resnikow, L. O. 30–31, 47
Rey, A. 13
Richards, I. A. 31
Ritchie, A. D. 31, 47
Robinson, W. P. 36, 47
Rossi-Landi, F. 48

Sampson, G. 36
Sapir, E. 44
Saussure, F. de 9, 11, 13–15, 18–19, 28, 34, 37, 43–45
Schaeffer, P. 18, 23
Schleidt, W. 43
Schlieben-Lange, B. 22, 24, 45
Searle, J. R. 24
Sebeok, Th. A. 45, 48
Shands, H. C. 45
Skinner, B. F. 44
Stockhausen, K. 47
Stokoe, W. C. 15–16, 38, 45

Templeton, W. B. 46

Vernon, M. D. 45–46

Walther, E. 13–14, 25, 33, 44, 47
Watzlawick, P. 45
Whitehead, A. N. 32
Whitfield, F. J. 44
Worth, S. 18–20
Wunderlich, D. 20, 38
Wundt, W. 17

Zipf, P. 44